Right Wing Poems:
Satirical Poetry

Roger Lance

Table of Contents

INTRODUCTION

Whimsical poems for all those on the right who are overwhelmed by the outright lies and stupidity of those on the left.

Roger Lance's writings provide a philosophical, historical and practical framework for revitalizing the conservative vision for American society. Right Wing Poems is a book of satirical poetry about the fanatical, liberal left wing politicians. As we stand in the midst of a liberal assault on constitution-based values, Lance's passionate conservatism shines through his satirical writing style and his keen observation of the world around us. As a strong supporter of common sense, His hilarious brand of realism is refreshing and necessary than ever.

Poor Sick Johnny

Johnny is a conservative
Who works on the hill,
One day he ate some liberal garbage
And became very ill.

Johnny went to his doctor
To find a cure,
Stay away from MSNBC
That's for sure.

So Johnny went home
And got into bed,
Took his doctors advice
Watched Fox news instead.

If you want to stay healthy
Wealthy and wise,
Don't swallow
Those liberal lies.

Tax and Spend

Tax tax tax
Spend spend spend,
To those on the left
There is no end.

Trillions in debt
Food stamps everywhere,
Those on the left
Just don't care.

Jobs are hard to find
Unemployment is high,
The left will not change
Until the day they die.

More On The Way!

Republic

This ole Republic
Is being torn apart,
By those Democratic voters
Who aren't very smart.

They vote for greed
They vote for perks,
They elect some
Of the biggest jerks.

One of these days
The Republic will be gone,
They will be the first to holler
What went wrong.

Holder Trash

Do you think Eric Holder
Will ever come clean,
Not in
Your wildest dream.

To him Fast and Furious
Is just a game,
Nothing will happen to him
In his office he will remain.

Now there is an attorney general
That should be in jail,
On contempt charges
Without any bail.

Take A Look

If you look on the left
What do you find,
Fat Democrat women
With big behinds.

Like Michelle Obama
With a big fat rear,
And her husband Barry
With big ole ears.

If you look on the right
What do you see,
Some of the prettiest women
As fit as can be.

No More Christmas

The left with their thinking
Makes me sick,
Who in their right mind
Wants to get rid of Saint Nick.

No more Merry Christmas
It's Happy Holidays now,
Who really cares
What they allow.

God is now gone
From the dollar and prayer,
Christianity will be banned
You better beware.

The next time a liberal
Says Happy Holidays to me,
I will attack them like
A Killer Bee.

No More Guns

Better hide your guns
Pack them safely away,
Soon they will be illegal
To own one day.

The left don't like them
They never will,
Soon more laws to regulate them
Will be on the hill.

If the left keeps going
The second amendment will be undone,
And soon it will be against the law
To own a gun.

No More Guns

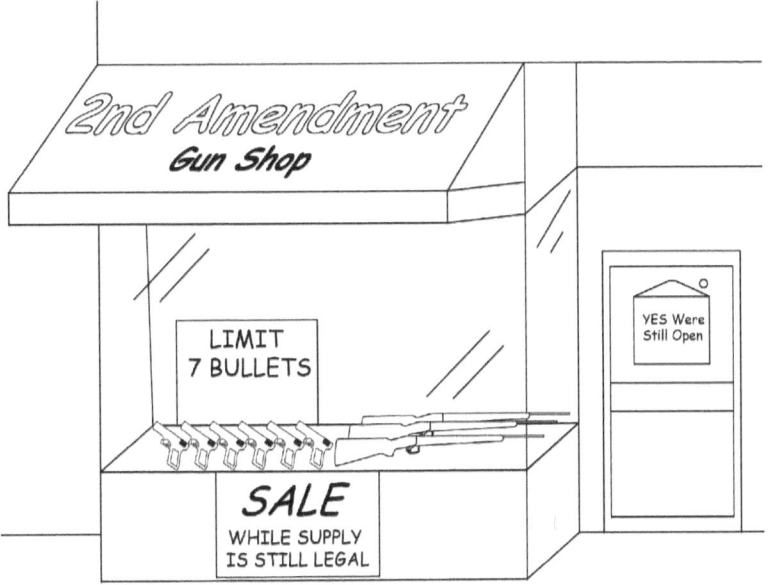

Family

My uncle is a RINO
My nephew is a queer
My aunt is a lesbian
Glad they don't live near.

My cousin voted for Obama
My niece thinks liberals are cool,
My whole family tree
Are a bunch of damn fools.

My wife is a conservative
And so am I,
We will stay that way
Until the day we die.

Four More

Well four more years
Michelle will have fun,
Flying here to there
On Air Force One.

Barry will try
To golf some more,
Trying to improve
His golfing score.

There will be more rappers
Coming through the White House door,
Lots of hip hop music
Gangsters dancing on the floor.

George Washington hanging on the wall
Will roll over in his grave,
After seeing how
Barry and Michelle behave.

Juggling

What are those liberals drinking
It must be over 140 proof,
Acting like drunken moonshiners
More pork spending through the roof.

The sorry bunch of liberals on the hill
Are nothing but a bunch of clowns,
They should be in the Ringling Brothers circus
As jugglers juggling their trillions around.

People paying to see their juggling act
Would soon see its nothing but a joke,
In just a short matter of time
The great circus would end up broke.

Liberal Clowns

Great Leaders

Their are some great leaders
Can you name one,
Well on the left
They got Sharpton.

Then there are the Clintons
A perfect couple of two,
Except when Monica is around
To screw.

Don't forget John Kerry
Secretary of State to dread,
With lots of ketchup
All over his bed.

Also Vice President Biden
Now there is a thrill,
The biggest comic
On capitol hill.

The left have great leaders
As you can plainly see,
They all have something in common
Like trash and debris.

Red Tape

You need to go talk
To my builder friend Sly,
Ask him how many
Permits he had to buy.

He decided to build
A tree house for his son,
He thought the project
Was going to be fun.

He was in his backyard
Getting ready to erect,
When a liberal government employee
Came by to collect.

He told him he needed a license
Permits, approval and more,
Then they would take it to a committee
For them to explore.

Sly abandoned his plans
No tree house no more,
His son soon discovered
The little conservative girl next door.

Son said to his dad
Be happy you saved money,
You didn't have to deal with permits
And I found me a honey.

Benghazi

Was it a video
That caused all the roar,
Or was it Muslims
Trying to even the score.

From what I have learned
Rice is a liar,
A terrorist attack
Started the fire.

Now that I know more
About the Benghazi attack,
The politicians on the left
Must be smoking crack.

Starting A Fire

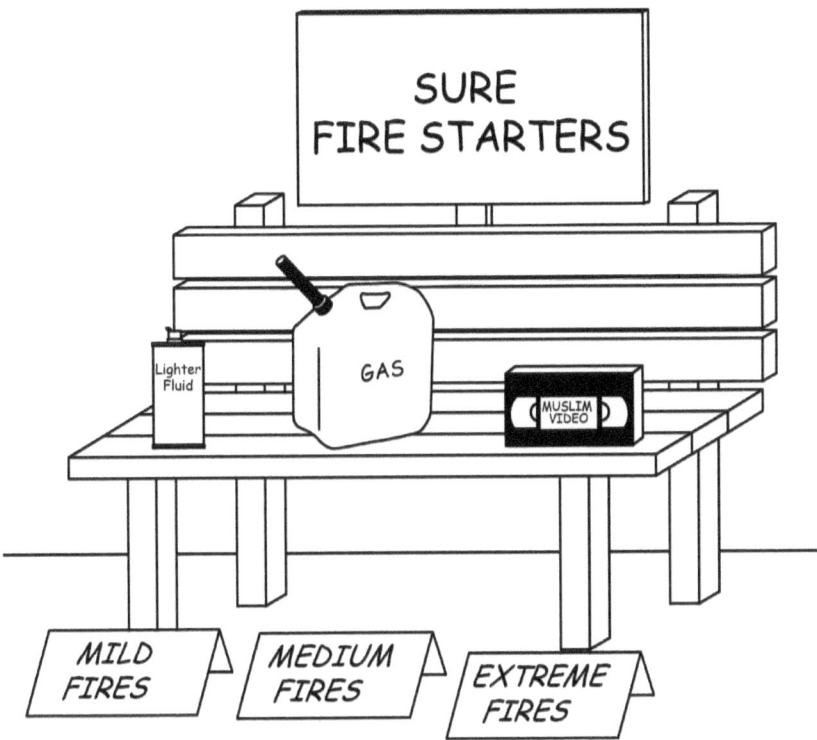

Rush

If it is the truth
You want to hear,
Turn on your radio
And open your ears.

There is one talk show host
Who will set you straight,
The one all the liberals
Seem to hate.

Tune into Rush
And listen for awhile,
Get updated on the facts
Take notes and compile.

Even if you are blue
You could always turn red,
You might even become
A ditto head.

School Prayer

No more prayer
In the local school,
They have replaced it
With a new kind of rule.

The rule of music
Where the children sing,
Praises of the new coming
Obama The King.

What Do I See

When looking at a forest
What does a liberal see,
Thousands of ways
To charge a government fee.

When looking at the gulf
What comes to a liberals mind,
Oil rigs and pollution
Of every kind.

When looking at a newborn baby
A liberal looks into his eyes,
Soon you will be drawing
Your SSI.

When I look at liberals
What do I see,
Deranged individuals
As goofy as can be.

Newborn Liberal Baby

Greatest President

Name the greatest President
Living or dead,
Which one
Comes to your head.

Ask the question to
Those college students today,
It is disturbing
What they will say.

Obama likes all gays
He lets them marry,
He is the greatest of them all
President Barry.

College students have been taught
In these great liberal schools,
They are all a bunch
Of uneducated fools.

Gone To Far

The feds keep printing money
It's not worth a dime,
It's all coming to a head
In a short matter of time.

The left wants a Socialist Nation
And President Barry agrees,
It will be a disaster epidemic
Greater than any disease.

There will be a revolution
Mayhem murder and strife,
You better get prepared
Or you will live a Socialist life.

God bless our Republic
The greatest nation around,
Please stop the left
From dragging us down.

Which Left

Which left lying blog
Lies the most,
Smart people know
It's the Huffington Post.

Which left newspaper
Is full of left slime,
It's one of the biggest
The New York Times.

Which left politician
Is the worst of its kind,
That is hard to answer
Hundreds come to my mind.

Crappy NY Times

Perfect Pair

Remember President Bill Clinton
All the girls he used to screw,
When he got in trouble with Monica
Jesse Jackson was there to pull him through.

Then Jackson complained that the right
Was trying to bring Clinton down,
He had a lot of room to talk
As he himself was screwing around.

Clinton and Jackson
Now there is two peas in a pod,
Not one moral between them
Now isn't that odd.

Illegal

I still don't know to this day
What the word illegal means,
To those on the left
It doesn't mean a hill of beans.

You got illegal aliens
Then there is illegal weed,
Instead of enforcing the laws
They decide to recede.

The more illegal aliens
And dope heads we got,
Means a lot more Democrats
In the melting pot.

Harry Reid

Listening to Harry Reid speak
With his artificial heart,
Just hearing him talk
You know he is not very smart.

He has got to be the most pathetic
Senator on the hill,
Unless it's pork and taxes
He will never pass a bill.

The people of Nevada
They are mighty dumb,
One day they will realize
He is nothing but pond scum.

Time To Take a Harry Reid

Happy New Year 2013

Well it's a New Year
And Barry is still in control,
Along with his buddy Reid
The perfect asshole.

Boehner still in control
A RINO to me,
He has common ground with Barry
A speaker he is not fit to be.

Secretary Clinton is now out
With a knot to her head,
Laying in a hospital wondering
Which girl is now in Bill's bed.

Spending still going on
Trillions and more,
The liberals don't care
When it comes to reform they will ignore.

It looks like four more years
Of the same ole crap,
It will be the Tea Party house members
Who will take all the rap.

MSM

Oh the main stream media
Now that is a group,
It never amazes me
How low they will stoop.

Lie after lie
Story after story,
Trying to promote socialism
For all its glory.

If you believe what they say
Or the stories they sell,
You will believe just about anything
A person has to tell.

Schumer

When I think of a whiner
Chuckie Schumer comes to my mind,
A pathetic person
Of the biggest kind.

When I think of a loser
Schumer is a big one,
The same rhetoric over and over
Reminds me of a rerun.

What a hippocratic person
The left always turns to,
Would you want a Senator like this
Representing you.

Liberals

The left can lie
And lie some more,
But I know
The real score.

I don't know
What the left doesn't get,
It seems the liberals
Don't give a shit.

Except when it comes
To their own personal gain,
Liberals are nothing but vultures
On a food chain.

Jackson & Sharpton

Jesse Jackson and Al Sharpton
There is a pair for you,
Two thugs acting like preachers
Hatred they spew.

Jackson and Sharpton
Two racist they are,
Running over the white race
Like a freight car.

Both of them have been caught
With their hand in the cookie jar,
For them to talk about morals and laws
Is extremely bizarre.

Executive Orders

Executive order here
Executive order there,
Executive orders of all kinds
Everywhere.

Forget congress enacting laws
To hell with the hobbit right wing,
Let me make it perfectly clear
I am the King.

Throw down your guns
I rule the land,
Executive order now
To take guns out of your hands.

Obama is the ruler
To hell with you and I,
Your rights are disappearing
In a blink of an eye.

The New Deal

Barry has a plan
To tax the rich,
Spend more money
Keep digging the ditch.

You can tell by his actions
He is one dumb fool,
If you could see his college records
He probably failed math in school.

Over sixteen trillion in debt
A few extra dollars on the way,
The crash is coming
It will be here any day.

No programs being cut
He wants to spend some more,
Soon China will put a stop
To the candy store.

No More China

Marriage

All the babies will be gone
In a few more years,
As the left is now promoting
The marriage of queers.

There will be daddy Bob
And mother Bill,
The left can quit giving
Out the pill.

Pretty Mary Ann
And butch Linda Lou,
That means traditional marriage
Is almost through.

Marriage License Bureau

Government Health

Are you over sixty five
And barely alive,
Wake up its plain and clear
Obamacare is near.

You will be told
You are too old,
It is time to fear
Government health care is near.

No more check ups
No more doctor care,
This is what you will be getting
With the new Obama Care.

Go Greg Go

If you watch Fox news
There is an interesting guy,
He is on early in the morning
The host of the Red Eye.

He is also on The Five
With some hot conservative chicks,
With his whimsical observations
Giving it to those liberal hicks.

His name is Greg Gutfeld
He has a great political insight,
A witty and talented person
Delivering liberal thrashings with delight.

Queer Scouts

I hear the Boy Scouts
Have changed their name,
It is now called Gay Scouts
Isn't that a shame.

Let your son join
And maybe one day,
He will become a Eagle Scout queer
And marry a gay.

The motto Be Prepared
Is no longer around,
BE PROUD is now their motto
Gay Scout leaders win hands down.

New Logo Design

I Forgot

Is Holder a
Black rot
Brown rot
Or dry rot
I forgot.

Is Clinton a
Love knot
Chip shot
A cannot
I forgot.

Is Biden a
Crack shot
Goof pot
What not
I forgot.

Is Pelosi a
Big shot
One shot
A blood clot
I forgot.

More often than not
They are all liberal snots
Bunch of distraughts
I haven't forgot.

Names Make Me Sick

Obama and Reid
Two jerks on the hill,
Just hearing their names
Makes me ill.

Pelosi and Frank
Now that is a pair,
Hearing them talk
I want to pull out my hair.

I can go on and on
Name after name,
But when I got done
I would be totally insane.

EPA

I went outside
And farted the other day,
The next thing I knew
I got a letter from the EPA.

They said my air
Was not very clear,
I said what the hell
And got me a beer.

I began to think
And drink more beer,
I then took their letter
And wiped my rear.

I put it in a envelope
And sent it first class,
Put a note on it
Stick it up your ass.

My Book

The left politician is getting more radical
Just take a closer look,
If they were doing this in private practice
They would be referred to as crooks.

With the left eroding the Constitution
With a smirk on their face,
To all you liberal politicians
You are a disgrace.

The left is going to complain
About my poems and my outlook,
Can you now do me a big favor
Tell your Right Wing friends to BUY MY BOOK!

The End

It is now time to go
This is the end,
Stay strong in your Conservative beliefs
Always be ready to defend.

**I hope some of my witty poems here
brought a smile to your face
and brightened your day.**

*If you would be so kind as to leave me
a review on Amazon about my book
or mention my book on your social
networks or on your website.*

Good Luck Stay Right!

Thank you for purchasing my little book.
May God Bless You.

Website: www.RogerLance.com

About the Author

Roger Lance, a native of the Midwest, has always had a flair for writing whimsical poetry. With a dedicated interest in conservative politics, His debut book, Right Wing Poems highlights his conservative beliefs and a vision of a world with limited government, less regulations, core family values and balanced budgets. He is a man who believes in the voice of reason. He possesses a great respect for our country and the legacy of our founding Fathers, which you will see reflected on every page.

www.ingramcontent.com/pod-product-compliance
Lightning Source LLC
Chambersburg PA
CBHW030535290526
45786CB00004B/1724